THE ANTIGONE OF SOPHOCLES

Another English Version by Dudley Fitts and Robert Fitzgerald

THE ALCESTIS OF EURIPIDES

THE ANTIGONE OF SOPHOCLES

AN ENGLISH VERSION
BY DUDLEY FITTS AND
ROBERT FITZGERALD

HARCOURT, BRACE AND COMPANY
NEW YORK

first edition

Designed by Robert Josephy

PRINTED IN THE UNITED STATES OF AMERICA

TO HORACE GREGORY

πολλὰ γάρ σε θεσπίζονθ' ὁρῶ
κοὐ ψευδόφημα

THE CHARACTERS REPRESENTED:

ANTIGONE
ISMENE
EURYDICE

CREON
HAIMON
TEIRESIAS

A SENTRY
A MESSENGER
CHORUS

SCENE: *Before the palace of Creon, King of Thebes. A central double door, and two lateral doors. A platform extends the length of the façade, and from this platform three steps lead down into the 'orchestra,' or chorus-ground. Time: dawn of the day after the repulse of the Argive army from the assault on Thebes.*

CONTENTS

PROLOGUE

[ANTIGONE *and* ISMENE *enter from the central door of the Palace.*

ANTIGONE:

Ismenê, dear sister,
You would think that we had already suffered enough
For the curse on Œdipus:
I cannot imagine any grief
That you and I have not gone through. And now—
Have they told you the latest decree of our King Creon?

ISMENE:

I have heard nothing: I know
That two sisters lost two brothers, a double death
In a single hour; and I know that the Argive army
Fled in the night; but beyond this, nothing.

ANTIGONE:

I thought so. And that is why I wanted you
To come out here with me. There is something we must do.

ISMENE:

Why do you speak so strangely?

ANTIGONE:

Listen, Ismenê:
Creon buried our brother Eteoclês
With military honours, gave him a soldier's funeral,
And it was right that he should; but Polyneicês,
Who fought as bravely and died as miserably,—
They say that Creon has sworn
No one shall bury him, no one mourn for him,
But his body must lie in the fields, a sweet treasure
For carrion birds to find as they search for food.

That is what they say, and our good Creon is coming here
To announce it publicly; and the penalty—
Stoning to death in the public square!
There it is,
And now you can prove what you are:
A true sister, or a traitor to your family.

ISMENE:

Poor Antigonê! But what can I do about it?

ANTIGONE:

You must decide whether you will help me or not.

ISMENE:

I don't understand you. Help you in what?

ANTIGONE:

Ismenê, I am going to bury him. Will you come?

ISMENE:

Bury him! You have just said the new law forbids it.

ANTIGONE:

He is my brother. And he is your brother, too.

ISMENE:

But think of the danger! Think what Creon will do!

ANTIGONE:

Creon is not strong enough to stand in my way.

ISMENE:

Ah sister!
Œdipus died, everyone hating him
For what his own search brought to light, his eyes
Ripped out by his own hand; and Iocastê died,
His mother and wife at once: she twisted the cords

That strangled her life; and our two brothers died,
Each killed by the other's sword. And we are left:
But oh, Antigonê,
Think how much more terrible than these
Our own death would be if we should go against Creon
And do what he has forbidden! We are only women,
We cannot fight with men, Antigonê!
The law is strong, we must give in to the law
In this thing, and in worse. I beg the Dead
To forgive me, but I am helpless: I must yield
To those in authority. And I think it is dangerous business
To be always meddling.

ANTIGONE:

If that is what you think,
I should not want you, even if you asked to come.
You have made your choice, you can be what you want to be.
But I will bury him; and if I must die,
I say that this crime is holy: I shall lie down
With him in death, and I shall be as dear
To him as he to me.

It is the dead,
Not the living, who make the longest demands:
We die for ever . . .

You may do as you like,
Since apparently the laws of the gods mean nothing to you.

ISMENE:

They mean a great deal to me; but I have no strength
To break laws that were made for the public good.

PÁRODOS

CHORUS:

Now the long blade of the sun, lying [STROPHE 1
Level east to west, touches with glory
Thebes of the Seven Gates. Open, unlidded
Eye of golden day! O marching light
Across the eddy and rush of Dircê's stream,
Striking the white shields of the enemy
Thrown headlong backward from the blaze of morning!

CHORAGOS:

Polyneicês their commander
Roused them with windy phrases,
He the wild eagle screaming
Insults above our land,
His wings their shields of snow,
His crest their marshalled helms.

CHORUS:

Against our seven gates in a yawning ring [ANTISTROPHE 1
The famished spears came onward in the night;
But before his jaws were sated with our blood,
Or pinefire took the garland of our towers,
He was thrown back; and as he turned, great Thebes—
No tender victim for his noisy power—
Rose like a dragon behind him, shouting war.

CHORAGOS:

For God hates utterly
The bray of bragging tongues;

And when he beheld their smiling,
Their swagger of golden helms,
The frown of his thunder blasted
Their first man from our walls.

CHORUS:

We heard his shout of triumph high in the air [STROPHE 2
Turn to a scream; far out in a flaming arc
He fell with his windy torch, and the earth struck him.
And others storming in fury no less than his
Found shock of death in the dusty joy of battle.

CHORAGOS:

Seven captains at seven gates
Yielded their clanging arms to the god
That bends the battle-line and breaks it.
These two only, brothers in blood,
Face to face in matchless rage,
Mirroring each the other's death,
Clashed in long combat.

CHORUS:

But now in the beautiful morning of victory [ANTISTROPHE 2
Let Thebes of the many chariots sing for joy!
With hearts for dancing we'll take leave of war:
Our temples shall be sweet with hymns of praise,
And the long night shall echo with our chorus.

I

CHORAGOS:

But now at last our new King is coming:
Creon of Thebes, Menoiceus' son.
In this auspicious dawn of his reign
What are the new complexities
That shifting Fate has woven for him?
What is his counsel? Why has he summoned
The old men to hear him?

[*Enter* CREON *from the Palace, C. He addresses the* CHORUS *from the top step.*

CREON:

Gentlemen: I have the honour to inform you that our Ship of State, which recent storms have threatened to destroy, has come safely to harbour at last, guided by the merciful wisdom of Heaven. I have summoned you here this morning because I know that I can depend upon you: your devotion to King Laïos was absolute; you never hesitated in your duty to our late ruler Œdipus; and when Œdipus died, your loyalty was transferred to his children. Unfortunately, as you know, his two sons, the princes Eteoclês and Polyneicês, have killed each other in battle; and I, as the next in blood, have succeeded to the full power of the throne.

I am aware, of course, that no Ruler can expect complete loyalty from his subjects until he has been tested in office. Nevertheless, I say to you at the very outset that I have nothing but contempt for the kind of Governor who is afraid, for whatever reason, to follow the course that he knows is best for the State;

and as for the man who sets private friendship above the public welfare,—I have no use for him, either. I call God to witness that if I saw my country headed for ruin, I should not be afraid to speak out plainly; and I need hardly remind you that I would never have any dealings with an enemy of the people. No one values friendship more highly than I; but we must remember that friends made at the risk of wrecking our Ship are not real friends at all.

These are my principles, at any rate, and that is why I have made the following decision concerning the sons of Œdipus: Eteoclês, who died as a man should die, fighting for his country, is to be buried with full military honours, with all the ceremony that is usual when the greatest heroes die; but his brother Polyneicês, who broke his exile to come back with fire and sword against his native city and the shrines of his fathers' gods, whose one idea was to spill the blood of his blood and sell his own people into slavery—Polyneicês, I say, is to have no burial: no man is to touch him or say the least prayer for him; he shall lie on the plain, unburied; and the birds and the scavenging dogs can do with him whatever they like.

This is my command, and you can see the wisdom behind it. As long as I am King, no traitor is going to be honoured with the loyal man. But whoever shows by word and deed that he is on the side of the State,—he shall have my respect while he is living, and my reverence when he is dead.

CHORAGOS:

If that is your will, Creon son of Menoiceus,
You have the right to enforce it: we are yours.

CREON:

That is my will. Take care that you do your part.

CHORAGOS:

We are old men: let the younger ones carry it out.

CREON:

I do not mean that: the sentries have been appointed.

CHORAGOS:

Then what is it that you would have us do?

CREON:

You will give no support to whoever breaks this law.

CHORAGOS:

Only a crazy man is in love with death!

CREON:

And death it is; yet money talks, and the wisest
Have sometimes been known to count a few coins too many.

[*Enter* SENTRY *from L.*

SENTRY:

I'll not say that I'm out of breath from running, King, because every time I stopped to think about what I have to tell you, I felt like going back. And all the time a voice kept saying, 'You fool, don't you know you're walking straight into trouble?'; and then another voice: 'Yes, but if you let somebody else get the news to Creon first, it will be even worse than that for you!' But good sense won out, at least I hope it was good sense, and here I am with a story that makes no sense at all; but I'll tell it anyhow, because, as they say, what's going to happen's going to happen, and—

CREON:

Come to the point. What have you to say?

SENTRY:

I did not do it. I did not see who did it. You must not punish me for what someone else has done.

CREON:

A comprehensive defence! More effective, perhaps,
If I knew its purpose. Come: what is it?

SENTRY:

A dreadful thing . . . I don't know how to put it—

CREON:

Out with it!

SENTRY:

Well, then;
The dead man—
Polyneicês—

[*Pause. The* SENTRY *is overcome, fumbles for words.* CREON *waits impassively.*

out there—
someone,—
New dust on the slimy flesh!

[*Pause. No sign from* CREON.

Someone has given it burial that way, and
Gone . . .

[*Long pause.* CREON *finally speaks with deadly control:*

CREON:

And the man who dared do this?

SENTRY:

I swear I
Do not know! You must believe me!
Listen:
The ground was dry, not a sign of digging, no,
Not a wheeltrack in the dust, no trace of anyone.
It was when they relieved us this morning: and one of them,
The corporal, pointed to it.
There it was,
The strangest—
Look:
The body, just mounded over with light dust: you see?
Not buried really, but as if they'd covered it
Just enough for the ghost's peace. And no sign
Of dogs or any wild animal that had been there.

And then what a scene there was! Every man of us
Accusing the other: we all proved the other man did it,
We all had proof that we could not have done it.
We were ready to take hot iron in our hands,
Walk through fire, swear by all the gods,
It was not I!
I do not know who it was, but it was not I!

[CREON'S *rage has been mounting steadily, but the* SENTRY *is too intent upon his story to notice it*

And then, when this came to nothing, someone said
A thing that silenced us and made us stare
Down at the ground: you had to be told the news,
And one of us had to do it! We threw the dice,
And the bad luck fell to me. So here I am,
No happier to be here than you are to have me:
Nobody likes the man who brings bad news.

CHORAGOS:

I have been wondering, King: can it be that the gods have done this?

CREON: [*Furiously*

Stop!
Must you doddering wrecks
Go out of your heads entirely? 'The gods!'
Intolerable!
The gods favour this corpse? Why? How had he served them?
Tried to loot their temples, burn their images,
Yes, and the whole State, and its laws with it!
Is it your senile opinion that the gods love to honour bad men?
A pious thought!—
No, from the very beginning
There have been those who have whispered together,
Stiff-necked anarchists, putting their heads together,
Scheming against me in alleys. These are the men,
And they have bribed my own guard to do this thing.

Money! [*Sententiously*
There's nothing in the world so demoralising as money.
Down go your cities,

Homes gone, men gone, honest hearts corrupted,
Crookedness of all kinds, and all for money!

[*To* SENTRY

But you—!

I swear by God and by the throne of God,
The man who has done this thing shall pay for it!
Find that man, bring him here to me, or your death
Will be the least of your problems: I'll string you up
Alive, and there will be certain ways to make you
Discover your employer before you die;
And the process may teach you a lesson you seem to have missed:
The dearest profit is sometimes all too dear:
That depends on the source. Do you understand me?
A fortune won is often misfortune.

SENTRY:

King, may I speak?

CREON:

Your very voice distresses me.

SENTRY:

Are you sure that it is my voice, and not your conscience?

CREON:

By God, he wants to analyse me now!

SENTRY:

It is not what I say, but what has been done, that hurts you.

CREON:

You talk too much.

SENTRY:

Maybe; but I've done nothing.

CREON:

Sold your soul for some silver: that's all you've done.

SENTRY:

How dreadful it is when the right judge judges wrong!

CREON:

Your figures of speech
May entertain you now; but unless you bring me the man,
You will get little profit from them in the end.

[*Exit* CREON *into the Palace.*

SENTRY:

'Bring me the man'—!
I'd like nothing better than bringing him the man!
But bring him or not, you have seen the last of me here.
At any rate, I am safe!

[*Exit* SENTRY

ODE I

CHORUS:

Numberless are the world's wonders, but none [STROPHE I
More wonderful than man; the stormgrey sea
Yields to his prows, the huge crests bear him high;
Earth, holy and inexhaustible, is graven
With shining furrows where his plows have gone
Year after year, the timeless labour of stallions.

[ANTISTROPHE I

The lightboned birds and beasts that cling to cover,
The lithe fish lighting their reaches of dim water,
All are taken, tamed in the net of his mind;
The lion on the hill, the wild horse windy-maned,
Resign to him; and his blunt yoke has broken
The sultry shoulders of the mountain bull.

Words also, and thought as rapid as air, [STROPHE 2
He fashions to his good use; statecraft is his,
And his the skill that deflects the arrows of snow,
The spears of winter rain: from every wind
He has made himself secure—from all but one:
In the late wind of death he cannot stand.

O clear intelligence, force beyond all measure! [ANTISTROPHE 2
O fate of man, working both good and evil!
When the laws are kept, how proudly his city stands!
When the laws are broken, what of his city then?
Never may the anárchic man find rest at my hearth,
Never be it said that my thoughts are his thoughts.

II

[*Re-enter* SENTRY *leading* ANTIGONE.

CHORAGOS:

What does this mean? Surely this captive woman
Is the Princess, Antigonê. Why should she be taken?

SENTRY:

Here is the one who did it! We caught her
In the very act of burying him.—Where is Creon?

CHORAGOS:

Just coming from the house.

[*Enter* CREON, *C.*

CREON:

What has happened?
Why have you come back so soon?

SENTRY: [*Expansively*

O King,
A man should never be too sure of anything: good warning
I would have sworn
That you'd not see me here again: your anger
Frightened me so, and the things you threatened me with;
But how could I tell then
That I'd be able to solve the case so soon?

No dice-throwing this time: I was only too glad to come!

Here is this woman. She is the guilty one:
We found her trying to bury him.

Take her, then; question her; judge her as you will.
I am through with the whole thing now, and glád óf it.

CREON:

But this is Antigonê! Why have you brought her here?

SENTRY:

She was burying him, I tell you!

CREON: *[Severely*

Is this the truth?

SENTRY:

I saw her with my own eyes. Can I say more?

CREON:

The details: come, tell me quickly!

SENTRY:

It was like this:

After those terrible threats of yours, King,
We went back and brushed the dust away from the body.
The flesh was soft by now, and stinking,
So we sat on a hill to windward and kept guard.
No napping this time! We kept each other awake.
But nothing happened until the white round sun
Whirled in the centre of the round sky over us:
Then, suddenly,
A storm of dust roared up from the earth, and the sky
Went out, the plain vanished with all its trees
In the stinging dark. We closed our eyes and endured it.
The whirlwind lasted a long time, but it passed;
And then we looked, and there was Antigonê!

I have seen
A mother bird come back to a stripped nest, heard
Her crying bitterly a broken note or two

For the young ones stolen. Just so, when this girl
Found the bare corpse, and all her love's work wasted,
She wept, and cried on heaven to damn the hands
That had done this thing.

And then she brought more dust
And sprinkled wine three times for her brother's ghost.

We ran and took her at once. She was not afraid,
Not even when we charged her with what she had done.
She denied nothing.

And this was a comfort to me,
And some uneasiness: for it is a good thing
To escape from death, but it is no great pleasure
To bring death to a friend.

Yet I always say
There is nothing so comfortable as your own safe skin!

CREON: [*Slowly, dangerously*

And you, Antigonê,
You with your head hanging,—do you confess this thing?

ANTIGONE:

I do. I deny nothing.

CREON: [*To* SENTRY:

You may go.

[*Exit* SENTRY

[*To* ANTIGONE:

Tell me, tell me briefly:
Had you heard my proclamation touching this matter?

ANTIGONE:

It was public. Could I help hearing it?

CREON:

And yet you dared defy the law.

ANTIGONE:

I dared.

It was not God's proclamation. That final Justice
That rules the world below makes no such laws.

Your edict, King, was strong,
But all your strength is weakness itself against
The immortal unrecorded laws of God.
They are not merely now: they were, and shall be,
Operative for ever, beyond man utterly.

I knew I must die, even without your decree:
I am only mortal. And if I must die
Now, before it is my time to die,
Surely this is no hardship: can anyone
Living, as I live, with evil all about me,
Think Death less than a friend? This death of mine
Is of no importance; but if I had left my brother
Lying in death unburied, I should have suffered.
Now I do not.

You smile at me. Ah Creon,
Think me a fool, if you like; but it may well be
That a fool convicts me of folly.

CHORAGOS:

Like father, like daughter: both headstrong, deaf to reason!
She has never learned to yield.

CREON:

She has much to learn.

The inflexible heart breaks first, the toughest iron
Cracks first, and the wildest horses bend their necks
At the pull of the smallest curb.

Pride? In a slave?

This girl is guilty of a double insolence,
Breaking the given laws and boasting of it.
Who is the man here,
She or I, if this crime goes unpunished?
Sister's child, or more than sister's child,
Or closer yet in blood—she and her sister
Win bitter death for this!

[*To servants:*

Go, some of you,

Arrest Ismenê. I accuse her equally.
Bring her: you will find her sniffling in the house there.

Her mind's a traitor: crimes kept in the dark
Cry for light, and the guardian brain shudders;
But how much worse than this
Is brazen boasting of barefaced anarchy!

ANTIGONE:

Creon, what more do you want than my death?

CREON:

Nothing.

That gives me everything.

ANTIGONE:

Then I beg you: kill me.

This talking is a great weariness: your words
Are distasteful to me, and I am sure that mine
Seem so to you. And yet they should not seem so:
I should have praise and honour for what I have done.
All these men here would praise me
Were their lips not frozen shut with fear of you.

[*Bitterly*

Ah the good fortune of kings,
Licensed to say and do whatever they please!

CREON:

You are alone here in that opinion.

ANTIGONE:

No, they are with me. But they keep their tongues in leash.

CREON:

Maybe. But you are guilty, and they are not.

ANTIGONE:

There is no guilt in reverence for the dead.

CREON:

But Eteoclês—was he not your brother too?

ANTIGONE:

My brother too.

CREON:

And you insult his memory?

ANTIGONE: [*Softly*

The dead man would not say that I insult it.

CREON:

He would: for you honour a traitor as much as him.

ANTIGONE:

His own brother, traitor or not, and equal in blood.

CREON:

He made war on his country. Eteoclês defended it.

ANTIGONE:

Nevertheless, there are honours due all the dead.

CREON:

But not the same for the wicked as for the just.

ANTIGONE:

Ah Creon, Creon,
Which of us can say what the gods hold wicked?

CREON:

An enemy is an enemy, even dead.

ANTIGONE:

It is my nature to join in love, not hate.

CREON: *[Finally losing patience*

Go join them, then; if you must have your love,
Find it in hell!

CHORAGOS:

But see, Ismenê comes:

[Enter ISMENE, *guarded*

Those tears are sisterly, the cloud
That shadows her eyes rains down gentle sorrow.

CREON:

You too, Ismenê,

Snake in my ordered house, sucking my blood
Stealthily—and all the time I never knew
That these two sisters were aiming at my throne!

Ismenê,

Do you confess your share in this crime, or deny it?
Answer me.

ISMENE:

Yes, if she will let me say so. I am guilty.

ANTIGONE: [*Coldly*

No, Ismenê. You have no right to say so.
You would not help me, and I will not have you help me.

ISMENE:

But now I know what you meant; and I am here
To join you, to take my share of punishment.

ANTIGONE:

The dead man and the gods who rule the dead
Know whose act this was. Words are not friends.

ISMENE:

Do you refuse me, Antigonê? I want to die with you:
I too have a duty that I must discharge to the dead.

ANTIGONE:

You shall not lessen my death by sharing it.

ISMENE:

What do I care for life when you are dead?

ANTIGONE:

Ask Creon. You're always hanging on his opinions.

ISMENE:

You are laughing at me. Why, Antigonê?

ANTIGONE:

It's a joyless laughter, Ismenê.

ISMENE:

But can I do nothing?

ANTIGONE:

Yes. Save yourself. I shall not envy you.
There are those who will praise you; I shall have honour, too.

ISMENE:

But we are equally guilty!

ANTIGONE:

No more, Ismenê.

You are alive, but I belong to Death.

CREON: [*To the* CHORUS:

Gentlemen, I beg you to observe these girls:
One has just now lost her mind; the other
Has obviously never had a mind to lose.

ISMENE:

Grief teaches the steadiest minds to waver, King.

CREON:

Yours certainly did, when you assumed guilt with the guilty!

ISMENE:

But how could I go on living without her?

CREON:

You are.

She is already dead.

ISMENE:

But your own son's bride!

CREON: [*Brutally*

There are places enough for him to push his plow.

I'll have no fanatic slut for my son's wife!

ISMENE:

O dearest Haimon, how your father wrongs you!

CREON:

I've had enough of your premature chatter of marriage!

CHORAGOS:

Do you really intend to steal this girl from your son?

CREON:

No; Death will do that for me.

CHORAGOS:

Then she must die?

CREON: [*Ironically*

You dazzle me.

—But enough of this talk!

[*To* GUARDS:

You, there, take them away and guard them well:
For they are but women, and even brave men run
When they see Death coming.

[*Exeunt* ISMENE, ANTIGONE, *and* GUARDS

ODE II

CHORUS: [STROPHE 1

Fortunate is the man who has never tasted God's vengeance!
Where once the anger of heaven has struck, that house is shaken
For ever: damnation rises behind each child
Like a wave cresting out of the black northeast,
When the long darkness under sea roars up
And bursts drumming death upon the windwhipped sand.

[ANTISTROPHE 1

I have seen this gathering sorrow from time long past
Loom upon Œdipus' children: generation from generation
Takes the compulsive rage of the enemy god.
So lately this last flower of Œdipus' line
Drank the sunlight! but now a passionate word
And a handful of dust have closed up all its beauty.

What mortal arrogance [STROPHE 2
Transcends the wrath of Zeus?
Sleep cannot lull him, nor the effortless long months
Of the timeless gods: but he is young for ever,
And his house is the shining day of high Olympos.
All that is and shall be,
And all the past, is his.
No pride on earth is free of the curse of heaven.

The straying dreams of men [ANTISTROPHE 2
May bring them ghosts of joy:
But as they drowse, the waking embers burn them;
Or they walk with fíxed éyes, as blind men walk.

But the ancient wisdom speaks for our own time:

Fate works most for woe
With Folly's fairest show.

Man's little pleasure is the spring of sorrow.

III

CHORAGOS:

But here is Haimon, King, the last of all your sons.
Is it grief for Antigonê that brings him here,
And bitterness at being robbed of his bride?

[*Enter* HAIMON

CREON:

We shall soon see, and no need of diviners.

—Son,

You have heard my final judgment on that girl:
Have you come here hating me, or have you come
With deference and with love, whatever I do?

HAIMON:

I am your son, father. You are my guide.
You make things clear for me, and I obey you.
No marriage means more to me than your continuing wisdom.

CREON:

Good. That is the way to behave: subordinate
Everything else, my son, to your father's will.
This is what a man prays for, that he may get
Sons attentive and dutiful in his house,
Each one hating his father's enemies,
Honouring his father's friends. But if his sons
Fail him, if they turn out unprofitably,
What has he fathered but trouble for himself
And amusement for the malicious?

So you are right

Not to lose your head over this woman.
Your pleasure with her would soon grow cold, Haimon,

And then you'd have a hellcat in bed and elsewhere.
Let her find her husband in Hell!
Of all the people in this city, only she
Has had contempt for my law and broken it.

Do you want me to show myself weak before the people?
Or to break my sworn word? No, and I will not.
The woman dies.

I suppose she'll plead 'family ties'. Well, let her.
If I permit my own family to rebel,
How shall I earn the world's obedience?
Show me the man who keeps his house in hand,
He's fit for public authority.
I'll have no dealings
With law-breakers, critics of the government:
Whoever is chosen to govern should be obeyed—
Must be obeyed, in all things, great and small,
Just and unjust! O Haimon,
The man who knows how to obey, and that man only,
Knows how to give commands when the time comes.
You can depend on him, no matter how fast
The spears come: he's a good soldier, he'll stick it out.

Anarchy, anarchy! Show me a greater evil!
This is why cities tumble and the great houses rain down,
This is what scatters armies!

No, no: good lives are made so by discipline.

We keep the laws then, and the lawmakers,
And no woman shall seduce us. If we must lose,
Let's lose to a man, at least! Is a woman stronger than we?

CHORAGOS:

Unless time has rusted my wits,
What you say, King, is said with point and dignity.

HAIMON: [*Boyishly earnest*

Father:
Reason is God's crowning gift to man, and you are right
To warn me against losing mine. I cannot say—
I hope that I shall never want to say!—that you
Have reasoned badly. Yet there are other men
Who can reason, too; and their opinions might be helpful.
You are not in a position to know everything
That people say or do, or what they feel:
Your temper terrifies them—everyone
Will tell you only what you like to hear.
But I, at any rate, can listen; and I have heard them
Muttering and whispering in the dark about this girl.
They say no woman has ever, so unreasonably,
Died so shameful a death for a generous act:
'She covered her brother's body. Is this indecent?
'She kept him from dogs and vultures. Is this a crime?
'Death?—She should have all the honour that we can give her!'

This is the way they talk out there in the city.

You must believe me:
Nothing is closer to me than your happiness.
What could be closer? Must not any son

Value his father's fortune as his father does his?
I beg you, do not be unchangeable:
Do not believe that you alone can be right.
The man who thinks that,
The man who maintains that only he has the power
To reason correctly, the gift to speak, the soul—
A man like that, when you know him, turns out empty.

It is not reason never to yield to reason!

In flood time you can see how some trees bend,
And because they bend, even their twigs are safe,
While stubborn trees are torn up, roots and all.
And the same thing happens in sailing:
Make your sheet fast, never slacken,—and over you go,
Head over heels and under: and there's your voyage.

Forget you are angry! Let yourself be moved!
I know I am young; but please let me say this:
The ideal condition
Would be, I admit, that men should be right by instinct;
But since we are all too likely to go astray,
The reasonable thing is to learn from those who can teach.

CHORAGOS:

You will do well to listen to him, King,
If what he says is sensible. And you, Haimon,
Must listen to your father.—Both speak well.

CREON:

You consider it right for a man of my years and experience
To go to school to a boy?

HAIMON:

It is not right

If I am wrong. But if I am young, and right,

What does my age matter?

CREON:

You think it right to stand up for an anarchist?

HAIMON:

Not at all. I pay no respect to criminals.

CREON:

Then she is not a criminal?

HAIMON:

The City would deny it, to a man.

CREON:

And the City proposes to teach me how to rule?

HAIMON:

Ah. Who is it that's talking like a boy now?

CREON:

My voice is the one voice giving orders in this City!

HAIMON:

It is no City if it takes orders from one voice.

CREON:

The State is the King!

HAIMON:

Yes, if the State is a desert.

[*Pause*

CREON:

This boy, it seems, has sold out to a woman.

HAIMON:

If you are a woman: my concern is only for you.

CREON:

God, your 'concern'! In a public brawl with your father!

HAIMON:

How about you, in a public brawl with justice?

CREON:

With justice, when all that I do is within my rights?

HAIMON:

You have no right to trample on God's right.

CREON: *[Completely out of control*

Fool, adolescent fool! Taken in by a woman!

HAIMON:

You'll never see me taken in by anything vile.

CREON:

Every word you say is for her!

HAIMON: *[Quietly, darkly*

And for you.

And for me. And for the gods under the earth.

CREON:

You'll never marry her while she lives.

HAIMON:

Then she must die.—But her death will cause another.

CREON:

Another?

Have you lost your senses? Is this an open threat?

HAIMON:

There is no threat in speaking to emptiness.

CREON:

By God, you'll regret this superior tone of yours!
You are the empty one!

HAIMON:

If you were not my father,
I'd say you were perverse.

CREON:

You girlstruck fool, don't play at words with me!

HAIMON:

I am sorry. You prefer blank silence.

CREON:

Now, by God—!
I swear, by all the gods in heaven above us,
You'll watch it, I swear you shall!

[*To the* SERVANTS:

Bring her out!
Bring the bitch out! Let her die before his eyes,
Here, this instant, with her bridegroom beside her!

HAIMON: [*Tiredly*

Not here, no; she will not die here, King.
And you will never see my face again.
Go on raving as long as you've a friend to endure you.

[*Exit* HAIMON

CHORAGOS:

Gone, gone.
Creon, a young man in a rage is dangerous!

CREON:

Let him do, or dream to do, more than a man can.
He shall not save these girls from death.

CHORAGOS:

These girls?

You have sentenced them both?

CREON:

No, you are right.

I will not kill the one whose hands are clean.

CHORAGOS:

But Antigonê?

CREON: [*Sombrely*

I will carry her far away
Out there in the wilderness, and lock her
Living in a vault of stone. She shall have food,
As the custom is, to absolve the State of her death.
And there let her pray to the gods of hell:
They are her only gods:
Perhaps they will show her an escape from death,
Or she may learn,

though late,

That piety shown the dead is pity in vain.

[*Exit* CREON

ODE III

CHORUS:

Love, unconquerable [STROPHE
Waster of rich men, keeper
Of warm lights and all-night vigil
In the soft face of a girl:
Sea-wanderer, forest-visitor!
Even the pure Immortals cannot escape you,
And mortal man, in his one day's dusk,
Trembles before your glory.

Surely you swerve upon ruin [ANTISTROPHE
The just man's consenting heart,
As here you have made bright anger
Strike between father and son—
And none has conquered but Love!
A girl's glánce wórking the will of heaven:
Pleasure to her alone who mocks us,
Merciless Aphroditê.

IV

CHORAGOS: [*As* ANTIGONE *enters guarded*

But I can no longer stand in awe of this,
Nor, seeing what I see, keep back my tears.
Here is Antigonê, passing to that chamber
Where all find sleep at last.

ANTIGONE:

Look upon me, friends, and pity me [STROPHE I
Turning back at the night's edge to say
Goodbye to the sun that shines for me no longer;
Now sleepy Death
Summons me down to Acheron, that cold shore:
There is no bridesong there, nor any music.

CHORUS:

Yet not unpraised, not without a kind of honour,
You walk at last into the underworld;
Untouched by sickness, broken by no sword.
What woman has ever found your way to death?

ANTIGONE:

How often I have heard the story of Niobê, [ANTISTROPHE I
Tantalos' wretched daughter, how the stone
Clung fast about her, ivy-close: and they say
The rain falls endlessly
And sifting soft snow; her tears are never done.
I feel the loneliness of her death in mine.

CHORUS:

But she was born of heaven, and you
Are woman, woman-born. If her death is yours,
A mortal woman's, is this not for you
Glory in our world and in the world beyond?

ANTIGONE:

You laugh at me. Ah, friends, friends, [STROPHE 2
Can you not wait until I am dead? O Thebes,
O men many-charioted, in love with Fortune,
Dear springs of Dircê, sacred Theban grove,
Be witnesses for me, denied all pity,
Unjustly judged! and think a word of love
For her whose path turns
Under dark earth, where there are no more tears.

CHORUS:

You have passed beyond human daring and come at last
Into a place of stone where Justice sits.
I cannot tell
What shape of your father's guilt appears in this.

ANTIGONE:

You have touched it at last: that bridal bed [ANTISTROPHE 2
Unspeakable, horror of son and mother mingling:
Their crime, infection of all our family!
O Œdipus, father and brother!
Your marriage strikes from the grave to murder mine.
I have been a stranger here in my own land:
All my life
The blasphemy of my birth has followed me.

CHORUS:

Reverence is a virtue, but strength
Lives in established law: that must prevail.
You have made your choice,
Your death is the doing of your conscious hand.

Greeks have a sense of moral responsibility and knows she determined her own fate; but still they have the idea of the fates ruling world.

ANTIGONE:

Then let me go, since all your words are bitter, [EPODE
And the very light of the sun is cold to me.
Lead me to my vigil, where I must have
Neither love nor lamentation; no song, but silence.

[CREON *interrupts impatiently*

CREON:

If dirges and planned lamentations could put off death,
Men would be singing for ever.

[*To the* SERVANTS:

Take her, go!
You know your orders: take her to the vault
And leave her alone there. And if she lives or dies,
That's her affair, not ours: our hands are clean.

ANTIGONE:

O tomb, vaulted bride-bed in eternal rock,
Soon I shall be with my own again
Where Persephonê welcomes the thin ghosts underground:
And I shall see my father again, and you, mother,
And dearest Polyneicês—
dearest indeed
To me, since it was my hand
That washed him clean and poured the ritual wine:
And my reward is death before my time!

And yet, as men's hearts know, I have done no wrong,
I have not sinned before God. Or if I have,

I shall know the truth in death. But if the guilt
Lies upon Creon who judged me, then, I pray,
May his punishment equal my own.

CHORAGOS:

O passionate heart,

Unyielding, tormented still by the same winds!

CREON:

Her guards shall have ample cause to regret their delaying.

ANTIGONE:

Ah, that voice has come very close to death!

CREON:

I will not deceive you by suggesting that you are mistaken.

ANTIGONE:

Thebes, and you my fathers' gods,
And rulers of Thebes, you see me now, the last
Unhappy daughter of a line of kings,
Your kings, led away to death. You will remember
What things I suffer, and at what men's hands,
Because I would not transgress the laws of heaven.

[*To the* GUARDS, *simply:*

Come: let us wait no longer.

[*Exit* ANTIGONE, *L., guarded*

ODE IV

CHORUS:

All Danaê's beauty was locked away [STROPHE 1
In a brazen cell where the sunlight could not come:
A small room, still as any grave, enclosed her.
Yet she was a princess too,
And Zeus in a rain of gold poured love upon her.
O child, child,
No power in wealth or war
Or tough sea-blackened ships
Can prevail against untiring Destiny!

And Dryas' son also, that furious king, [ANTISTROPHE 1
Bore the god's prisoning anger for his pride:
Sealed up by Dionysos in deaf stone,
His madness died among echoes.
So at the last he learned what dreadful power
His tongue had mocked:
For he had profaned the revels,
And fired the wrath of the nine
Implacable Sisters that love the sound of the flute.

And old men tell a half-remembered tale [STROPHE 2
Of horror done where a dark ledge splits the sea
And a double surf beats on the gréy shóres:
How a king's new woman, sick
With hatred for the queen he had imprisoned,
Ripped out his two sons' eyes with her bloody hands
While grinning Arês watched the shuttle plunge
Four times: four blind wounds crying for revenge,

Crying, tears and blood mingled.—Piteously born,
Those sons whose mother was of heavenly birth!
Her father was the god of the North Wind
And she was cradled by gales,
She raced with young colts on the glittering hills
And walked untrammeled in the open light:
But in her marriage deathless Fate found means
To build a tomb like yours for all her joy.

V

[*Enter blind* TEIRESIAS, *led by a boy. The opening speeches of* TEIRESIAS *should be in singsong contrast to the realistic lines of* CREON.

TEIRESIAS:

This is the way the blind man comes, Princes, Princes,
Lock-step, two heads lit by the eyes of one.

CREON:

What new thing have you to tell us, old Teiresias?

TEIRESIAS:

I have much to tell you: listen to the prophet, Creon.

CREON:

I am not aware that I have ever failed to listen.

TEIRESIAS:

Then you have done wisely, King, and ruled well.

CREON:

I admit my debt to you. But what have you to say?

TEIRESIAS:

This, Creon: you stand once more on the edge of fate.

CREON:

What do you mean? Your words are a kind of dread.

TEIRESIAS:

Listen, Creon:
I was sitting in my chair of augury, at the place
Where the birds gather about me. They were all a-chatter,
As is their habit, when suddenly I heard
A strange note in their jangling, a scream, a
Whirring fury; I knew that they were fighting,
Tearing each other, dying

In a whirlwind of wings clashing. And I was afraid.
I began the rites of burnt-offering at the altar,
But Hephaistos failed me: instead of bright flame,
There was only the sputtering slime of the fat thigh-flesh
Melting: the entrails dissolved in grey smoke,
The bare bone burst from the welter. And no blaze!

This was a sign from heaven. My boy described it,
Seeing for me as I see for others.

I tell you, Creon, you yourself have brought
This new calamity upon us. Our hearths and altars
Are stained with the corruption of dogs and carrion birds
That glut themselves on the corpse of Œdipus' son.
The gods are deaf when we pray to them, their fire
Recoils from our offering, their birds of omen
Have no cry of comfort, for they are gorged
With the thick blood of the dead.

O my son,

These are no trifles! Think: all men make mistakes,
But a good man yields when he knows his course is wrong,
And repairs the evil. The only crime is pride.

Give in to the dead man, then: do not fight with a corpse—
What glory is it to kill a man who is dead?
Think, I beg you:
It is for your own good that I speak as I do.
You should be able to yield for your own good.

CREON:

It seems that prophets have made me their especial province.
All my life long
I have been a kind of butt for the dull arrows
Of doddering fortune-tellers!
No, Teiresias:
If your birds—if the great eagles of God himself
Should carry him stinking bit by bit to heaven,
I would not yield. I am not afraid of pollution:
No man can defile the gods.
Do what you will,
Go into business, make money, speculate
In India gold or that synthetic gold from Sardis,
Get rich—you will not buy my consent to bury him.
Teiresias, it is a sorry thing when a wise man
Sells his wisdom, lets out his words for hire!

TEIRESIAS:

Ah Creon! Is there no man left in the world—

CREON:

To do what?—Come, let's have the aphorism!

TEIRESIAS:

No man who knows that wisdom outweighs any wealth?

CREON:

As surely as bribes are baser than any baseness.

TEIRESIAS:

You are sick, Creon! You are deathly sick!

CREON:

As you say: it is not my place to challenge a prophet.

TEIRESIAS:

Yet you have said my prophecy is for sale.

CREON:

The generation of prophets has always loved gold.

TEIRESIAS:

The generation of kings has always loved brass.

CREON:

You forget yourself! You are speaking to your King.

TEIRESIAS:

I know it. You are a king because of me.

CREON:

You have a certain skill; but you have sold out.

TEIRESIAS:

King, you will drive me to words that—

CREON:

Say them, say them!

Only remember: I will not pay you for them.

TEIRESIAS:

No, you will find them too costly.

CREON:

No doubt. Speak:

Whatever you say, you will not change my will.

TEIRESIAS:

Then take this, and take it to heart!

The day is not far off when you shall pay back

Corpse for corpse, flesh of your own flesh.

You have thrust the child of this world into living night,

You have kept from the gods below the child that is theirs:

The one in a grave before her death, the other,

example of antithesis

Dead, denied the grave. This is your crime:
And the Furies and the dark gods of Hell
Are swift with terrible punishment for you.

Do you want to buy me now, Creon?

Not many days,
And your house will be full of men and women weeping,
And curses will jostle you on every hand
For sons you have kept from burial in far cities
Sick with the stench of your insolence.

These are my arrows, Creon: they are all for you.

But come, child: lead me home. [*To* BOY:
Let him waste his fine anger upon younger men.
Maybe he will learn at last
To control a wiser tongue in a better head.

[*Exit* TEIRESIAS

CHORAGOS:
The old man has gone, King, but his words
Remain to plague us. I am old, too,
But I cannot remember that he was ever false.

CREON:
That is true. . . . It troubles me.
Oh it is hard to give in! but it is worse
To risk everything for stubborn pride.

groundwork before in the play for this change

CHORAGOS:
Creon: take my advice.

CREON:

What shall I do?

CHORAGOS:

Go quickly: free Antigonê from her tomb
And build a tomb for the body of Polyneicês.

CREON:

You would have me do this?

CHORAGOS:

Creon, yes!

And it must be done at once: God moves
Swiftly to cancel the folly of stubborn men.

CREON:

It is hard to deny the heart! But I
Will do it: I will not fight with destiny.

CHORAGOS:

You must go yourself, you cannot leave it to others.

CREON:

I will go.

—Bring axes, servants:

Come with me to the tomb. I buried her, I
Will set her free.

Oh quickly!

My mind misgives—
The laws of the gods are mighty, and a man must serve them
To the last day of his life!

[*Exit* CREON

PÆAN

CHORAGOS:

God of many names [STROPHE I

CHORUS:

O Iacchos

son

of Cadmeian Sémelê

O born of the Thunder!

Guardian of the West

Regent

of Eleusis' plain

O Prince of mænad Thebes

and the Dragon Field by rippling Ismenos:

CHORAGOS:

God of many names [ANTISTROPHE I

CHORUS:

the flame of torches

flares on our hills

the nymphs of Iacchos

dance at the spring of Castalia:

from the vine-close mountain

come ah come in ivy:

Evohé evohé! sings through the streets of Thebes

CHORAGOS:

God of many names [STROPHE 2

CHORUS:

Iacchos of Thebes
heavenly Child
of Sémelê bride of the Thunderer!
The shadow of plague is upon us:
come
with clement feet
oh come from Parnasos
down the long slopes
across the lamenting water

CHORAGOS:

Iô Fire! Chorister of the throbbing stars! [ANTISTROPHE 2
O purest among the voices of the night!
Thou son of God, blaze for us!

CHORUS:

Come with choric rapture of circling Mænads
Who cry *Iô Iacche!*
God of many names!

ÉXODOS

[*Enter* MESSENGER, *L.*

MESSENGER:

Men of the line of Cadmos, you who live
Near Amphion's citadel:
I cannot say
Of any condition of human life 'This is fixed,
This is clearly good, or bad'. Fate raises up,
And Fate casts down the happy and unhappy alike:
No man can foretell his Fate.
Take the case of Creon:
Creon was happy once, as I count happiness:
Victorious in battle, sole governor of the land,
Fortunate father of children nobly born.
And now it has all gone from him! Who can say
That a man is still alive when his life's joy fails?
He is a walking dead man. Grant him rich,
Let him live like a king in his great house:
If his pleasure is gone, I would not give
So much as the shadow of smoke for all he owns.

CHORAGOS:

Your words hint at sorrow: what is your news for us?

MESSENGER:

They are dead. The living are guilty of their death.

CHORAGOS:

Who is guilty? Who is dead? Speak!

MESSENGER:

Haimon.
Haimon is dead; and the hand that killed him
Is his own hand.

CHORAGOS:

His father's? or his own?

MESSENGER:

His own, driven mad by the murder his fat[illegible]

CHORAGOS:

Teiresias, Teiresias, how clearly you saw it[illegible]

MESSENGER:

This is my news: you must draw what [illegible]
from it.

CHORAGOS:

But look: Eurydicê, our Queen:
Has she overheard us?

[*Enter* EURYDIC[illegible]

EURYDICE:

I have heard something, friends:
As I was unlocking the gate of Pallas' sh[illegible]
For I needed her help today, I heard a vo[illegible]
Telling of some new sorrow. And I fain[illegible]
There at the temple with all my maiden[illegible]
But speak again: whatever it is, I can be[illegible]
Grief and I are no strangers.

MESSENGER:

Dearest La[illegible]

I will tell you plainly all that I have see[illegible]
I shall not try to comfort you: what is [illegible]
Since comfort could lie only in what is [illegible]
The truth is always best.

I went with [illegible]

[*Enter* MESSENGER, *L.*

MESSENGER:

Men of the line of Cadmos, you who live
Near Amphion's citadel:
I cannot say
Of any condition of human life 'This is fixed,
This is clearly good, or bad'. Fate raises up,
And Fate casts down the happy and unhappy alike:
No man can foretell his Fate.
Take the case of Creon:
Creon was happy once, as I count happiness:
Victorious in battle, sole governor of the land,
Fortunate father of children nobly born.
And now it has all gone from him! Who can say
That a man is still alive when his life's joy fails?
He is a walking dead man. Grant him rich,
Let him live like a king in his great house:
If his pleasure is gone, I would not give
So much as the shadow of smoke for all he owns.

CHORAGOS:

Your words hint at sorrow: what is your news for us?

MESSENGER:

They are dead. The living are guilty of their death.

CHORAGOS:

Who is guilty? Who is dead? Speak!

MESSENGER:

Haimon.
Haimon is dead; and the hand that killed him
Is his own hand.

CHORAGOS:

His father's? or his own?

MESSENGER:

His own, driven mad by the murder his father had done.

CHORAGOS:

Teiresias, Teiresias, how clearly you saw it all!

MESSENGER:

This is my news: you must draw what conclusions you can from it.

CHORAGOS:

But look: Eurydicê, our Queen:
Has she overheard us?

[*Enter* EURYDICE *from the Palace, C.*

EURYDICE:

I have heard something, friends:
As I was unlocking the gate of Pallas' shrine,
For I needed her help today, I heard a voice
Telling of some new sorrow. And I fainted
There at the temple with all my maidens about me.
But speak again: whatever it is, I can bear it:
Grief and I are no strangers.

MESSENGER:

Dearest Lady,
I will tell you plainly all that I have seen.
I shall not try to comfort you: what is the use,
Since comfort could lie only in what is not true?
The truth is always best.

I went with Creon

took easier course Pol. could not speak back.

To the outer plain where Polyneicês was lying,
No friend to pity him, his body shredded by dogs.
We made our prayers in that place to Hecatê
And Pluto, that they would be merciful. And we bathed
The corpse with holy water, and we brought
Fresh-broken branches to burn what was left of it,
And upon the urn we heaped up a towering barrow
Of the earth of his own land.

When we were done, we ran
To the vault where Antigonê lay on her couch of stone.
One of the servants had gone ahead,
And while he was yet far off he heard a voice
Grieving within the chamber, and he came back
And told Creon. And as the King went closer,
The air was full of wailing, the words lost,
And he begged us to make all haste. 'Am I a prophet?'
He said, weeping, 'And must I walk this road,
'The saddest of all that I have gone before?
'My son's voice calls me on. Oh quickly, quickly!
'Look through the crevice there, and tell me
'If it is Haimon, or some deception of the gods!'

We obeyed; and in the cavern's farthest corner
We saw her lying:
She had made a noose of her fine linen veil
And hanged herself. Haimon lay beside her,
His arms about her waist, lamenting her,
His love lost under ground, crying out
That his father had stolen her away from him.

When Creon saw him the tears rushed to his eyes
And he called to him: 'What have you done, child? Speak to me.
'What are you thinking that makes your eyes so strange?
'O my son, my son, I come to you on my knees!'
But Haimon spat in his face. He said not a word;
But his eyes—
And suddenly he drew his sword
And lunged. Creon shrank back, the blade missed; and the boy,
Desperate against himself, drove it half its length
Into his own side, and fell. And as he died
He gathered Antigonê close in his arms again,
Choking, his blood bright red on her white cheek.
And now he lies dead with the dead, and she is his
At last, his bride in the houses of the dead.

[*Exit* EURYDICE *into the Palace*

CHORAGOS:

She has left us without a word. What can this mean?

MESSENGER:

It troubles me, too; yet she knows what is best,
Her grief is too great for public lamentation,
And doubtless she has gone to her chamber to weep
For her dead son, leading her maidens in his dirge.

CHORAGOS:

It may be so: but I fear this deep silence.

[*Pause*

MESSENGER:

I will see what she is doing. I will go in.

[*Exit* MESSENGER *into the Palace*

[*Enter* CREON *with attendants, bearing* HAIMON'S *body*

CHORAGOS:

But here is the King himself: oh look at him,
Bearing his own damnation in his arms.

CREON:

Nothing you say can touch me any more.
My own blind heart has brought me
From darkness to final darkness. Here you see
The father murdering, the murdered son—
And all my civic wisdom!

Haimon my son, so young, so young to die,
I was the fool, not you; and you died for me.

CHORAGOS:

That is the truth; but you were late in learning it.

CREON:

This truth is hard to bear. Surely a god
Has crushed me beneath the hugest weight of heaven,
And driven me headlong a barbaric way
To trample out the thing I held most dear.

The pains that men will take to come to pain!

[*Enter* MESSENGER *from the Palace*

Whatever my hands have touched has come to nothing.
Fate has brought all my pride to a thought of dust.

[As CREON *is being led into the house, the* CHORAGOS *advances and speaks directly to the audience*

CHORAGOS:

There is no happiness where there is no wisdom;
No wisdom but in submission to the gods.
Big words are always punished,
And proud men in old age learn to be wise.

Pride

good epigram

Antigone had incredible intellectual integrity. - simple character relatively to modern works.

Choruses lead in + out of spoken interludes.

COMMENTARY

Et quod propriè dicitur in idiomate Picardorum horrescit apud Burgundos, immò apud Gallicos viciniores; quanto igitur magis accidet hoc apud linguas diversas! Quapropter quod bene factum est in unâ linguâ non est possibile ut transferatur in aliam secundum ejus proprietatem quam habuerit in priori.

ROGER BACON

I

In the Commentary appended to our version of Euripides' *Alcestis* we wrote: 'Our object was to make the *Alcestis* clear and 'credible in English. Since it is a poem, it had to be made clear as a 'poem; and since it is a play, it had to be made credible as a play. 'We set for ourselves no fixed rules of translation or of dramatic 'verse: often we found the best English equivalent in a literalness 'which extended to the texture and rhythm of the Greek phrasing; 'at other times we were forced to a more or less free paraphrase in 'order to achieve effects which the Greek conveyed in ways impos-'sible to English. Consequently, this version of the *Alcestis* is not 'a "translation" in the classroom sense of the word. The careful 'reader, comparing our text with the original, will discover altera-'tions, suppressions, expansions—a word, perhaps, drawn out into a 'phrase, or a phrase condensed to a word: a way of saying things 'that is admittedly not Euripidean, if by Euripidean one means a 'translation *ad verbum expressa* of Euripides' poem. In defense we 'can say only that our purpose was to reach—and, if possible, to 'render precisely—the emotional and sensible meaning in every 'speech in the play; we could not follow the Greek word for word, 'where to do so would have been weak and therefore false.' We have been guided by the same principles in making this version of the *Antigonê*.

II

We have made cuts only when it seemed absolutely necessary. The most notable excision is that of a passage of sixteen lines beginning with 904 (Antigonê's long speech near the end of Scene IV), which has been bracketed as spurious, either in whole or in part, by the best critics. Aristotle quotes two verses from it, which proves, as Professor Jebb points out, that if it is an interpolation it must have been made soon after Sophocles' death, possibly by his son Iophon. However that may be, it is dismal stuff. Antigonê is made to interrupt her lamentation by a series of limping verses whose sense is as discordant as their sound. We quote the Oxford Translation, the style of which is for once wholly adequate to the occasion:

'And yet, in the opinion of those who have just sentiments, I 'honoured you [Polyneicês] aright. For neither, though I had 'been the mother of children, nor though my husband dying, had 'mouldered away, would I have undertaken this toil against the 'will of the citizens. On account of what law do I say this? 'There would have been another husband for me if the first died, 'and if I lost my child there would have been another from 'another man! but my father and my mother being laid in the 'grave, it is impossible a brother should ever be born to me. On 'the principle of such a law, having preferred you, my brother, 'to all other considerations, I seemed to Creon to commit a sin, 'and to dare what was dreadful. And now, seizing me by force,

'he thus leads me away, having never enjoyed the nuptial bed,
'nor heard the nuptial lay, nor having gained the lot of marriage,
'nor of rearing my children; but thus I, an unhappy woman,
'deserted by my friends, go, while alive, to the cavern of the
'dead.'

There are other excisions of less importance. Perhaps the discussion of one of them will serve to explain them all. Near the end of the *Éxodos,* Creon is told of his wife's suicide. The Messenger has five very graphic lines describing Eurydicê's suicide, to which Creon responds with an outburst of dread and grief; yet two lines later, as if he had not heard the first time, he is asking the Messenger how Eurydicê died. The Messenger replies that she stabbed herself to the heart. There is no evidence that the question and reply are interpolations: on the contrary, they serve the definite purpose of filling out the iambic interlude between two lyric strophes; but in a modern version which does not attempt to reproduce the strophic structure of this *Kommós* they merely clog the dialogue. Therefore we have skipped them; and the occasional suppression of short passages throughout the play is based upon similar considerations.

III

In a like manner, we have not hesitated to use free paraphrase when a literal rendering of the Greek would result in obscurity. Again, the discussion of a specific instance may illuminate the whole question.

After Antigonê has been led away to death, the Chorus, taking a hint from her having compared her own fate to that of Niobê, proceeds to elaborate the stories of mythological persons who have suffered similar punishment. The Fourth Ode cites Danaê, Lycurgos, the son of Dryas, and Cleopatra, the daughter of Boreas and wife of the Thracian king of Phineus. Only Danaê is mentioned by name; the others are allusively identified. The difficulty arises from the allusive method: Sophocles' audience would be certain to recognize the allusions, but that is not true of ours. To what extent can we depend upon the audience's recognition in a day when, to quote Mr I. A. Richards, 'we can no longer refer with any confidence to any episode in the Bible, or to any nursery tale or any piece of mythology'? We can assume that the story of Danaê is still current; but Lycurgos is forgotten now, and the sordid Phineus-Cleopatra-Eidothea affair no longer stirs so much as an echo. Nevertheless, Sophocles devotes two of his four strophes to this Cleopatra, and he does it in so oblique a manner that 'translation' is out of the question. We have therefore rendered these strophes with such slight additions to the Greek sense as might convey an equivalent suggestion of fable to a modern audience.

IV

The Chorus is composed, says the Scholiast, of 'certain old men of Thebes': leading citizens ('O men many-charioted, in love with Fortune') to whom Creon addresses his fatal decree, and from whom he later takes advice. Sophocles' Chorus numbered fifteen, including the Choragos, or Leader; its function was to chant the Odes and, in the person of the Choragos, to participate in the action. In a version designed for the modern stage certain changes are inevitable. It cannot be urged too strongly that the words of the Odes must be intelligible to the audience; and they are almost certain not to be intelligible if they are chanted in unison by so large a group, with or without musical accompaniment. It is suggested, then, that in producing this play no attempt be made to follow the ancient choric method. There should be no dancing. The *Párodos,* for example, should be a solemn but almost unnoticeable evolution of moving or still patterns accompanied by a drum-beat whose rhythm may be derived from the cadence of the Ode itself. The lines given to the Chorus in the Odes should probably be spoken by single voices. The only accompaniment should be percussion: we follow Allan Sly's score of the *Alcestis* in suggesting a large side drum from which the snares have been removed, to be struck with two felt-headed tympani sticks, one hard, one soft.

V

A careful production might make successful use of masks. They should be of the Benda type used in the production of O'Neill's *The Great God Brown:* lifelike, closely fitting the contours of the face, and valuable only as they give the effect of immobility to character. On no account should there be any attempt to reproduce the Greek mask, which was larger than life size and served a function non-existent on the modern stage—the amplification of voice and mood for projection to the distant seats of the outdoor theatre.

If masks are used at all, they might well be allotted only to those characters who are somewhat depersonalized by official position or discipline: Creon, Teiresias, the Chorus and Choragos.

possibly the Messenger. By this rule, Antigonê has no mask; neither has Ismenê, Haimon, nor Eurydicê. If Creon is masked, we see no objection, in art or feeling, to the symbolic removal of his mask before he returns with the dead body of his son.

WE CANNOT let our *Antigonê* go without expressing our gratitude to those friends who have been so helpful to us in many ways: to Eleanor Green and Horace Gregory and Arthur Mizener for their acute criticism; to Margaret Goodwin, whose theatre-sense has been the relentless corrective of our poetry; and to Lydia Hewitt for the patience with which she made revision upon revision in the task of preparing the final manuscript.

DF

RF

All Souls' Day : 1938